The Fundraising Co-Pilot

A comprehensive guide for board members, volunteers, and fundraising professionals to fundraising programs that work!

Marc Huber

THE FUNDRAISING CO-PILOT

Copyright © 2016 by Marc Huber.

All rights reserved. No part of this book may be used or reproduced in any manner whatsoever without written permission except in the case of brief quotations embodied in critical articles or reviews.

For more information, contact:
Marc Huber
Fishers, IN 46038
marc@fundraisingcopilot.com
www.fundraisingcopilot.com

First Edition: November 2016

Table of Content

Introduction 4

The Basics

   Let's Get Started...7

   Your Toolkit 13

Elements of a Comprehensive Fundraising Program

   Building a Foundation: Your Annual Fund 25

   Stepping It Up: Major Gifts..41

   Comprehensive Fundraising: Planned Giving 52

   Corporate Gifts: What's In It for Them?..............................57

   Grant Writing: Foundations Have the Money? 63

   Government Grants..69

   A Word on Capital Campaigns 71

The People Who Make it all Work

   Working With Your Board 81

   Working with Volunteers...90

   Special Events 93

   Generational Fundraising 97

   Let's Talk Marketing 102

   Your Fundraising Staff 106

   Working with Consultants 112

Final Thoughts..117

About the Author 120

Introduction

Whether you're a supporter of a nonprofit, a board member, volunteer, or paid staff member, at some point you will hear about the need of the organization to raise money, or be recruited to support the fundraising effort. Asking others for money is an idea that many people are not entirely comfortable with – but there are ways to talk about fundraising and implement fundraising programs that can make the process much more accessible and even enjoyable.

I believe that most people dislike the idea of fundraising because they view it as a form of begging. They believe that they are somehow putting the other person out by asking them for money. Over these next few chapters, I will show you that fundraising is something worth doing with pride, and something that everybody can do. Being involved with fundraising allows you to help advance a cause you care deeply about. Good fundraising creates opportunities to share the mission of an organization with others. Through fundraising, we can invite others to create new opportunities for individuals, better our community, and improve the world around us. It is truly something to feel good about.

I have been involved with fundraising since 1998: from processing gifts, to running mail and phone campaigns, to making personal requests for five and six-figure gifts. With this book, I am hoping to share some of the "nuts and bolts" that make up a good fundraising program, and outline techniques and strategies that have proven successful.

Most of all, I hope this book will inspire you to invite others to share in your passion and your favorite cause.

The Basics

Let's Get Started

This chapter is the big one. This is where it all begins, where we define why we do what we do – as fundraisers, as board members and volunteers, or as members of the staff. If you don't read any other chapter besides this one, that's alright. No other chapter will be as important.

It all begins with the mission of your organization. Everything we do, we do because of our mission, and everything we *don't do* is also because of our mission. It defines our goal as well as our boundaries. Both are critical: one provides guidance and direction, the other prevents mission creep – meaning it keeps the organization from taking on activities that aren't really in line with its core mission. Mission creep or deviation from our core values can result in loss of focus and support.

There are different approaches to a good mission statement. Some say it needs to be short enough so everyone can memorize and readily repeat it. Others say it ought to be as long as it needs to be. No matter the length, a good mission statement includes two key components: a defined goal or objective (what the organization tries to achieve), and the core belief or beliefs that drives the effort.

As much as the mission of an organization has the potential to engage donors, it can also turn them away. That's okay. We want to engage donors who are just as excited about and invested in our cause as we are. If someone does not share the same values or has no interest in what we are trying to do, then it benefits no one to spend time engaging with them. That makes the mission statement the perfect filter to help us identify the people we really want to connect with: it becomes addition by subtraction. You don't waste time, energy, and resources on individuals who are unmoved by your cause, and who would not give regardless of the circumstances.

As a fundraiser (paid or volunteer), it is important to have this conversation with the director and key leaders about what the main objective and the core beliefs of the organization are. Is the main goal or objective well-defined? Are you able to paraphrase it and still get to the essence of it ("We at Little Angels Animal Shelter are trying to…", "What we want for the students at Kensington College is…")?

Next comes a clarification of the organization's core belief: why we do what we do. Start with the mission objective, and ask a series of *So what?* questions. (If it works better for you or your organization, feel free to substitute *So what?* with **Why?**)

The first few questions will be easy. After that, the exercise becomes a bit more challenging and thought-provoking. Asking these questions can be hard, but it is absolutely essential for every fundraiser to go through this process, because these are the same questions every potential donor – consciously or subconsciously – will have.

Let's use a campaign for a building expansion as an example:

- "We want to build a new expansion to our 80 year-old library. " – *So what?*
- "Because our community has grown and the new building no longer meets the needs of our patrons. It's too small and not wheelchair accessible." – *So what?*
- "Being able to provide adequate library services to all people in our community is critical, because we are the only resource like it within a 40 mile radius." – *So what?*
- "People need library services and access to the resources we offer." – *So what?*
- "Because public libraries can provide essential resources and information to individuals and families who might not otherwise have access to them." – *So what?*
- "Equitable access to resources and information helps create more opportunities for everyone." – *So what?*

- "Giving everyone more opportunities means they can grow as individuals. That's good for them, and for our community." – *So what?*

We can continue to drill down further, but what should become clear by now is that the conversation has moved away from something specific (building a library expansion) to something more abstract and universal (self-fulfillment, stronger communities).

In this particular case, libraries remove barriers and provide access to information, learning, and knowledge. The core belief that drives libraries is that access to information helps people learn and grow, and that this kind of access should be a public good. Anyone willing to seek information to learn and grow should be able to do so, and it should not be limited to only those with money or special privileges. By democratizing access to resources and information, libraries can have a very positive impact on the lives of people in their communities.

This is a core value that fosters understanding and appreciation of the organization at a much deeper level. It presents learning as a value, and it presents personal growth through knowledge as a value. Both of those values are universally relatable, and help position the organization in a much broader context for potential donors.

That's the first step. By going through this exercise, we can answer for ourselves the question *why* organizations like ours *need* to exist. Why do we need libraries? Why do we need universities? Homeless shelters? Food banks? Free health clinics? Museums? Community theater? Public radio?

While it may seem obvious at first glance ("Of course people love free community theater!"), it really is critical to work through this process, ideally in a small group, and articulate the need for an organization like ours to exist in very clear terms. Going through this process and *making it your own* will set the foundation you need to effectively ask for support and involvement in person, and to communicate the needs of the organization in a variety of ways.

The second step is even more important. First, we establish why there is a general need for an organization like ours ("Why are food banks important?"). Then we move on to answer that question very specifically: why does *our* organization need to exist in *our* community? ("Why is the East Middleton food bank important?").

Both questions work in tandem, and both are designed to address two very distinct purposes: helping you internalize and articulate the funding need of the organization, and helping overcome donor objections. Being able to articulate the funding need will make you a more effective spokesperson for your organization.

Being able to address donor objections may seem like something to only worry about in face-to-face fundraising, but in fact it needs to be present in all materials, including marketing and general communication pieces. Any piece of print communication needs to be approached as a dialogue with a potential donor. Anticipate potential questions or concerns to reader may have, and address them proactively. Carrying the same message, the same vision, and the same core beliefs throughout all communications and interactions is the foundation of a successful fundraising program.

Your Toolkit

The following components, policies, and documents will be very helpful when it comes to managing and guiding your organization to overall success. Especially if you are joining a nonprofit as a new board member, campaign chair, or staff at the leadership level, these items should be at the top of your list to inquire about and review.

If you find that any of these documents are not readily available or that some of these discussions have not taken place in some time, make them a priority during the first few weeks in your new role. Some of them will provide a better sense of purpose and direction while others may be crucial for legal reasons.

- **SWOT Analysis:** Have a strategic conversation with other leaders and board members about the strengths, weaknesses, opportunities, and threats for the organization. What does the organization do well? What does it not do well? How do its strengths or weaknesses support or hurt efforts to accomplish strategic goals?
Analyzing strengths and weaknesses is an internal assessment, whereas opportunities and threats are a careful review of the marketplace and the environment. In some

cases, there can be crossover: a small donor pool can be a weakness, but a large number of currently non-giving visitors, subscribers, or members can be a huge opportunity. A large revenue stream from the Annual Fund can be a strength, but if 50% of it is the result of a single generous donor, it could be a potential weakness.

There isn't a right or wrong way to conduct a SWOT analysis. The most important thing is that the process is done as objectively as possible. It can be a tough discussion to have, but it is absolutely necessary in order to direct all the energies to the right activities in the right order of priority. For that reason, it can be helpful to have an outside, neutral party come in to host a retreat, and moderate and capture the SWOT analysis discussion.

- **Strategic Plan:** Most organizations will have a five or ten year strategic plan. If you have been invited to join the board of directors, play a leadership role in a capital campaign, or join the staff at the leadership level, ask to see a copy of the strategic plan. Determine where in the plan the organization is at, and ask questions about the progress to date. Were any milestones missed? Why? Do milestones or intended outcomes now need to be adjusted? What changes are being made to ensure that the organization can catch up to any objectives it may be in danger of failing to achieve?

Not having a strategic plan isn't necessarily a problem. Having a strategic plan and not meeting objectives also isn't necessarily a problem. For example, there could have been an unexpected change at the CEO position in the previous year. The executive search required to fill that position may have caused the board to temporarily put other strategic plans objectives on hold. The response you get to your follow-up questions about the strategic plan will determine if this should raise any red flags.

- **Infrastructure:** Does the organization have a reliable database to house donor contact information and giving data? Does the donor database allow for pledge tracking? Does the system allow for accurate financial reports in a timely manner? How flexible and capable is data reporting and data analysis in general? Is donor data secure? How are gifts being processed and who handles bank deposits? Is there a clear separation between the person handling accounts payable and the person handling accounts receivable?

The later questions are more of a concern for board members who are ultimately responsible for the financial well-being of the organization. Having a reliable donor database will be of interest to volunteers involved in fundraising. Now they can ask for gift commitments knowing that donors won't be over-solicited, and that any pledges will get the appropriate followed-up. This gives volunteer fundraisers additional trust and confidence in your overall fundraising program.

- **Are you legal:** This one seems obvious, but especially for small or recently established nonprofits this can be an easily overlooked detail: in addition to earning nonprofit status from the Internal Revenue Service, some states require nonprofits to additionally register at the state level in order to be able to solicit donations. This is a step above and beyond earning 501(c)(3) tax exempt status and filing the 990 Return of Organization Exempt From Income Tax form – and it's not necessarily widely published or known. Often, that registration is also filed with a different office than the one that will receive the organization's annual tax return. I recommend visiting the website of the National Council of Nonprofits for a place to start. Additionally, you can visit the website of the Attorney General or the Secretary of State in the state where the nonprofit is headquartered to double-check potential registration requirements. It is worth noting that some states require nonprofits to be registered with them even if the organization is not headquartered there. If you plan on soliciting donors who live in a neighboring state, your organization may be required to be registered both in its home state *and* in that neighboring state. Some states require this registration to be renewed on an annual basis, and there may be filing fees. If you are invited to join a Board of Directors of a nonprofit, this is worth inquiring about before making the commitment to serve in that capacity.

- **Gift Acceptance Policy:** There are two reasons why having a gift acceptance policy is important: it helps the organizations figure out in advance how to take in and process certain gifts should they come about (and determine if the organization has the ability and capacity to accept particular types of gifts), and also to determine what kinds of gifts the organization cannot or will not accept.

The "cannot accept" part is probably easily accomplished in an open discussion with your board of directors, or a fundraising and financial advisory committee. Review all potential scenarios how a donor might make a gift (cash, check, credit card, gifts of publically traded stock, gifts of closely held stock, gifts of property, gifts of real estate, retirement plans, life insurance policies, time shares, annuities, copyrights, royalties, mining rights, etc.) and in consult with a legal advisor to determine what would need to be in place to accept each type of gift. Cash, checks, and credit cards are likely going to be easy. Gifts of publically traded stock may require setting up a brokerage account first. However, if there isn't an expectation of regular gifts of stock, is the organization prepared to pay ongoing fees just in case? It gets infinitely more complex with gifts of real estate, or large personal property. In some case, like with closely held stock or time shares, the organization may opt to not even accept them in the first place. All different giving vehicles should be discussed, and then adopted or rejected via board resolution.

Another aspect of the gift acceptance policy is that it is meant to help the organization navigate potential ethical, moral, or administrative issues before a gift is even considered. On an administrative level, the organization may opt to turn down gifts that would require the creation of an endowment where the principal gift amount is so low that the cost of administering it would far outweigh any potential returns. For that reason, some nonprofits adopt policies specifying minimum contribution levels for new endowments, funds, or initiatives.

Ethical or moral questions can be even stickier, and in those cases having a written gift acceptance policy handy can have tremendous benefits. Let's say your nonprofit is an urban homeless shelter with a strong focus on helping homeless families with children. A donor approaches you with the promise of a seven figure gift, but the stipulation is that the homeless shelter opens a new facility dedicated exclusively to the care of abandoned animals. While generous and thoughtful, the gift clearly falls outside the scope of the mission of the homeless shelter. After a long conversation, the donor decides to make the gift in support of the mission of your shelter. But there is a catch: the donor will only make the gift if the board agrees that only white families can stay at the shelter. You reject this restriction outright and state that your organization would only accept the donor's gift if there are no restrictions on who is eligible for services. The donor agrees and informs you that the gift will be made in the form of several shares of stock. Two days later, you receive a call from the donor's broker. During the conversation, the broker informs you that the shares of stock are from a company that has recently made headlines for making huge profits off of child labor, with children as young as nine working over 50 hours a week. Knowing that, do you still accept the gift? If you do, how would the community and local media respond?

Using a gift acceptance policy to settle those ethical issues in advance of any potential gift is essential. It gives fundraisers guidelines to share with potential donors, and it can protect the organization from consequences that could be devastating to its reputation and its legal and financial standing. These are not the discussions a board needs to have the moment a seven-figure gift is looming. These considerations need to be made in advance, and from a non-emotional and level-headed perspective. Everything should be put in writing and adopted by the board as official policy. The board should routinely review (every three to five year) all policies, and if necessary make the appropriate changes.

- **Stewardship plan:** At the most basic level, the stewardship plan lays out what happens after a gift has been received. It establishes guidelines how quickly the organization should create and send acknowledgement letters (ideally the same day), and who within the organization should sign them. In addition, there can be other prescribed activities: gifts over $500 may prompt a thank-you call from the organization's Executive Director, and gifts over $1,000 may prompt a personal thank-you call from a member of the board of directors. Your organization may opt to do similar activities at higher giving amounts, or incorporate additional tasks. Your organization may also choose to establish an annual honor roll of donors where donors at higher levels of giving receive greater public recognition. The purpose of a stewardship plan is to provide guidance and enforce consistency. In addition, a stewardship plan can help with the budgeting of stewardship activities, especially if special events – like donor recognition dinners – are being considered. Lastly, the stewardship plan can be used to outline permanent recognition opportunities, such as naming facilities, naming programs, or naming endowments. For the benefit of the organization and the donor, it is advisable to determine minimum contribution levels where necessary, and to have clear guidelines in writing under what conditions a naming opportunity may be revoked in the future.

- **Communication plan:** Regular communication about your nonprofit can help lay the groundwork for bringing in new volunteers and potential donors. It can promote a general understanding of the mission and the work you do in your community, making it more likely to have productive gift conversations with donors. Having active communication channels will also allow you to address negative news about the organization more readily and effectively. Just in case, it may be necessary to identify emergency or crisis communication plans well in advance. If there is an incident at your facility, who will address the media and when? For more serious issues, does the organization have an external communications manager identified they might be able to call on?

Knowing when, how much, and how frequently to put out content on your website, newsletters, news releases, and social media will help you better gauge the time commitment necessary to do so, and whether or not this might adversely affect the time and resources needed for effective fundraising. You may determine that either your fundraising or your communication plan is overly ambitious. This can allow you to re-prioritize, or develop a case for additional staff or volunteer support.

The role of a good communication plan also plays a big part in your donor recognition efforts. As rule of thumb, donors should be thanked for their gift seven times or more before another request for support is made. Those seven thank-yous don't need to be seven letters from the Executive Director. Recognizing donors on your website, in newsletters, or other publications also works well. Having a timetable for regular communications will allow you to incorporate donor recognition opportunities throughout the year.

- **Investment plan:** An investment plan lays out how the organization will manage its assets, in particular its endowment. This may not be something worth worrying about for smaller organizations with very modest revenue streams, but as soon as there are predictable operating surpluses or the organization is in the position to set-up its first endowment, an investment policy needs to be considered by the board. It will spell out how short-term investments are to be handled, and how long-term investments and endowment payouts are to occur. With endowments, some organizations opt to reinvest part of the interest earned back into the core endowment principal to help protect it against inflation. It is a consideration worth making, but it also means that in the short term the money available to the organization will be diminished.

Having clearly spelled out investment policies and practices is a benefit to donors. It signals that the organization is thoughtful about the gifts it receives, and is looking and planning for the future. The donor knows that their money will be wisely invested, and will be able to trust that the organization will adhere to the donor's wishes for how the money is to be spent. Trust between donor and the nonprofit is essential. An intentional and thoughtful investment plan is a foundation of that trust.

Elements of a Comprehensive Fundraising Program

Building a Foundation: Your Annual Fund

Every year, the bulk of all charitable giving (over 80%) comes from individuals. As a result, successful fundraising programs always focus on individual donors first. Donors typically progress through stages of increasing connectedness and support of the organization. In the beginning, they are identified by the organization and asked to make their first gift. A large number of donors will only make a one-time gift, so it is essential for organizations to engage them and ensure a repeat donation.

Eventually, loyal donors may choose to upgrade their regular annual gift, and subsequently decide to make a special gift to a specific initiative or program. A small number of contributors have the ability and the interest to eventually give a major gift, and a select few may choose to include the organization in their will by making a planned gift (often resulting in their largest gift ever).

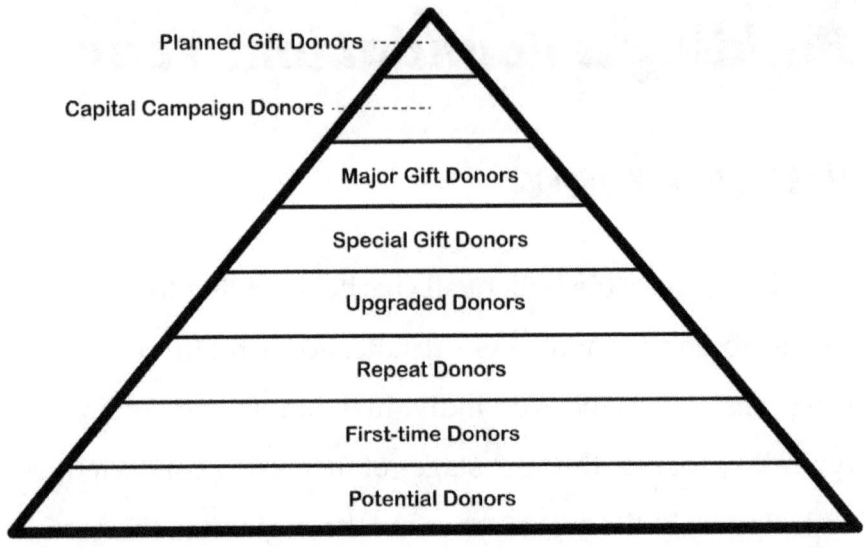

Not all donors will eventually get to the point of making an estate gift, and not all donors necessarily start at the very bottom of this pyramid. However this kind of model, by large, is true for the majority of donors, especially those who do become major supporters. The main reason for introducing the donor pyramid in the Annual Fund section is the key role the Annual Fund plays in any successful fundraising program: while necessary to cover general operating expenses, it is also a pipeline to develop large donations from individuals in subsequent years.

For the purpose of this chapter, I will focus on the Annual Fund as a way for an organization to raises money for ongoing budget expenses. Money can be raised by mail, email, telephone, in person, bake sale, silent auction, raffles (which may require additional registrations), golf outings, and so on. Some nonprofits depend greatly on the performance of their Annual Fund. If certain revenue targets aren't being met, the services offered may need to be scaled back or stopped altogether.

Very few nonprofits have the luxury of treating their Annual Fund like it's icing on the cake. For most, it's a means of survival. If you are just joining a nonprofit as a fundraiser or board member, the role and make-up of the Annual Fund should be one of the first things to take a look at. Few things will give you a better indicator of the overall health of the organization. How big of a share of the organization's annual revenue does the Annual Fund represent? Are there aspects of the Annual Fund that are dominant contributors, for example does the organization host one special event each year which produces the lion share of its annual operating revenue? If 80% of the annual budget depends on one successful charity event on the local golf course, what is the potential impact if that event gets rained out, or does not pan out as planned?

Even if the Annual Fund is a good blend of different solicitation approaches (combining mailings, digital fundraising, and in-person asks), are there particular factors that could spell disaster for the organization down the road?

There are some smaller organizations that depend heavily on the generosity of a small number of deeply invested supporters. What would happen if one of them decided to scale their donation of $50,000 a year down to $5,000? Could your organization carry on?

The Annual Fund can provide a lot of answers about the viability and growth potential of the organization. If you are asked to take on significant responsibilities as a volunteer (join the board, help raise significant gifts for a campaign), or if you are considering joining the organization as a member of the professional fundraising staff, this is one area where asking the right questions can be of vital importance.

The Role of the Annual Fund

In the world of fundraising, the Annual Fund is often the "non-sexy" stream of contributions when compared to major gifts. Major gifts let donors name buildings and endowments, and have the potential to move an organization forward in a very significant way. That said, a well-managed Annual Fund can be one of the most important success factors of a nonprofit. Here is why:

- With very few exceptions, the majority of major gift donors of an organization start by making an initial modest contribution. If your Annual Fund is under-resourced, there is a very real potential that in time the support through major donors will dry up. The Annual Fund is both a foundation and a pipeline for sustained major gift support down the road.

- Very regular contributors of modest annual gifts have an enormous potential to leave a gift for the organization in their estate. Anyone who has given in eight or more years over the last decade should be considered a primary candidate for including your organization in their will. These gifts do not need to be very large: anyone who has given $100 each year for ten years in a row should be on the short list of individuals to discuss an estate gift with.
- If your nonprofit is serious about launching a capital campaign, a core component of any feasibility study will be a review of the Annual Fund. First-time annual donations are frequently impulse gifts. How sound and consistent an organization's fundraising performance is will be reflected in the percentage of donors who renew their support on an annual basis.

Major gifts and capital campaign gifts typically come primarily from an organization's most loyal and invested supporters, which only occur after careful consideration by the donor and their family. Engaging a high capacity donor often begins by connecting them to the organization with a first gift to the Annual Fund.

Elements of a Comprehensive Annual Fund

There are a multitude of ways for organizations to secure donations on an annual basis: by mail, by phone (this is especially the case for colleges and universities), by email and through social media, in-person, and through special events or activities like raffles, auctions, and so on.

A well-managed Annual Fund will use a variety of strategies and approaches to address differences in generational giving habits, and to prevent the organization from placing all eggs into one basket.

Let's look at the different giving vehicles along with their pros and cons.

- **Mail Appeals:** Mail appeals still continue to perform quite well, especially among older donors. A mail appeal allows nonprofits to share a substantial amount of information with the donor. It is also the least intrusive. The donor can respond how and when they want, whether to send a check, call, or make a gift online. Mailings can be outsourced fairly easily, allowing even small organizations to effectively connect with hundreds of supporters.

One downside is cost: while mail appeals usually perform very well with the right audience, it requires a certain critical mass before it swings into high profitability. The cost of producing stationary, envelopes, reply envelopes, pledge cards, and brochures drops dramatically when the number of recipients goes up from 1,000 to 10,000. When an organization is just starting out, in-house donor lists of 10,000 contacts or more are rare. That is why growing the database and always acquiring new prospects is critical for any nonprofit.

A successful mail appeal program will rely on segmentation and testing. Having one standard letter for every recipient is simply not enough. Regular donors need one customized message, returning donors need another, and potential donors who have yet to make their first gift need a different letter altogether. The key to a good mailing is personalization. The donor needs to feel that the letter was written just for them, and that the organization knows them at a personal level. For example, a donation request letter that begins with the words "Dear Friend" should be avoided at all costs. At a minimum, it should be personalized, outline an urgent need, and ask the recipient for a specific amount to contribute.

Secondly, if the donor list is large enough to gather meaningful data, it is good to occasionally test different strategies. Do donors respond better if the mailing is in a non-standard envelope? Is there a better response rate if the outer envelope has an actual stamp instead of the postage meter imprint? Do photos on the envelope make a difference? While segmenting the mailing list is a requirement, testing different strategies from time to time has the potential to really optimize your mailing, and set it apart from all the other appeals that donors receive in their mailbox.

- **Phone campaigns:** Phone-a-thons can be incredibly successful under the right conditions and for the right organization. For colleges and universities, phone-a-thons work great. The main issue with phone campaigns is that they are very labor intensive. Many universities outsource their phone-a-thon to professional telemarketing companies, because engaging tens of thousands of alumni in a short period of time is extraordinarily challenging. This type of outsourcing comes at a price, sometimes in the five to six figure range. The logistical requirements and up-front costs can make phone-a-thons for small to mid-sized organizations impractical as a fundraising tool. That said, there are three ways a phone-a-thon can work for organizations of any size:

- The Thank-a-thon: this is a great way to engage board members and leadership volunteers. Ask them to spend some time just making thank-you calls to donors. Donors typically love this kind of special attention, and hearing from appreciative donors tends to leave board members and volunteers with strong positive feelings about the organization. That's a win-win for everyone.
- Engaging with significant supporters: when the end of the fiscal year comes around and some of the most significant and generous donors still have not made their annual gift, a personal call from the CEO, a board member, or the fundraising staff can help secure those critical, larger gifts. Even if those efforts fail, it is a good way to pay some extra attention to the organization's most loyal donors. If there are any issues with the organization, the donor now has the immediate attention of someone who may be able to help address their concerns.
- Membership drives: this does not apply to all organizations, but some nonprofits (zoos, performing arts organizations) depend on annual subscribers or ticket holders, and for those purposes host annual membership or subscriber renewal drives. In those cases, it is possible to request a donation at the time the renewal call is made.

- **Digital fundraising:** While online fundraising has grown a lot in recent years, it is still not quite the dominant force some of us in the nonprofit sector had expected it to be (in political fundraising, online giving has very much arrived). But make no mistake: nonprofits cannot afford to ignore digital fundraising, even if initial results don't seem promising. There is a generational shift taking place that increases both donor trust and donor expectations in digital giving. Digital fundraising needs to be broken down into two categories: email and social media. Email is still the undisputed leader. On average, people check their email far more frequently than any social media platform, and email accounts are still being created in greater numbers than social media accounts. Email is an incredibly efficient and cost effective way to communicate with donors and supporters. Even if you have no immediate plans to launch a significant online fundraising effort, there are two things you must absolutely do: collect as many email addresses from donors and potential supporters as you can, and get their permission to reach out to them via email. Over time, you can test the occasional email appeal and monitor responses.

  The other aspect of digital fundraising is social media. Social media platforms change their tools, rules, and guidelines so frequently that it would be futile to discuss any of them here at length. My personal take is that donors may expect you to be in a certain social media environment, but if you aren't and otherwise connecting with them sufficiently, that's generally acceptable. However, if you choose to have a presence on social media (Facebook, Snapchat, Twitter, Instagram, etc.), then do commit to it. Merely creating an account is not good enough. Develop a general communications plan and stick to it. Don't leave your social media platforms unattended. It is better to only select a few and do those well than try to cover as many as possible while managing them poorly.

The two most important things digital outreach and social media can do for you are: collecting the email addresses of your supporters and securing permission to contact them. Digital fundraising has one great strength which is also its biggest weakness: encouraging impulse-driven gifts. Every time a major disaster makes the news, there is a significant spike in online giving. People want to help, and they want to help *immediately*. There is no time for a carefully crafted mail appeal to get written, edited, designed, printed, and mailed, arriving weeks after the fact. Digital fundraising is at its best when it functions as a rapid response, or when it gets swept up in a viral messaging effort like the Ice Bucket Challenge to help fight Amyotrophic Lateral Sclerosis (ALS or Lou Gehrig's disease). However, because those campaigns are largely impulse-driven, they rarely result in follow-up gifts. The year after the Ice Bucket Challenge, donations to The ALS Society reverted back to levels much closer to where they were before the Ice Bucket Challenge took off. Rather than hoping to capture lightning in a bottle, the key to digital fundraising at your organization should be to organically increase your base of donors and followers with opt-in permissions, and to augment your other fundraising efforts with a complementary online effort.

The biggest headache social media and digital fundraising will cause is data security. While donors are becoming more comfortable making gifts online, it is up to your organization to make absolutely certain that their data and their giving records are protected. Few things would damage the relationship with your donors more than getting their financial data compromised. It is imperative that if you choose to solicit contributions online the process is as secure as it can possibly be.

- **Special events:** Special events are a double-edged sword. They can bring in large amounts of money, but often the effort can put extraordinary demands on resources and staff time. By the time everything is accounted for, including the cost of work hours spent making the event a success, it needs to be evaluated really carefully if hosting the event is truly worth it. I have witnessed colleagues argue successfully that their time is better used meeting with a few major donors than to spent weeks planning and executing one single event.

Some major events may be unavoidable. Schools and universities will always want to host alumni reunions. Some organizations see special events as a way to engage board members and supporters, and to reach out to the community. Those are very valid reasons, but if those are important goals of the organization, there need to be strategies in place to leverage the event accordingly.

Special events can also serve an important function in thanking donors. Those kinds of events would not directly impact annual fundraising efforts and should be viewed as donor stewardship and recognition activities.

While the cost per dollar raised is easy to determine with mail, phone, and online campaigns, that issue can become very muddled with special events. I encourage any organization to look at the total picture of any special event. If it becomes clear that the event is a net asset to the organization, keep doing it. If it's basically a break-even operation as a fundraiser, it may be time to try other alternatives.

- **In-person solicitations:** Some annual gifts do need to be treated as major gifts, and in those cases it's best to take the time to connect with the donor in person rather than "invoicing" them by mail. The impact of major gifts on your Annual Fund should not be overlooked. In those cases, requesting a donation in person is absolutely the right thing to do.

Building the Annual Fund

Annual giving is a constant ebb and flow of donors. Each year, a brand new donor will make their very first gift to your organization while another donor, who may have contributed for five years straight, decides to redirect their gift to a different charity. Successful Annual Fund programs always pay attention to the following:

- **Addressing donor attrition:** The organization must find a way to always bring in new donors, whether that is reconnecting with lapsed donors (your best prospects), volunteers, program participants or beneficiaries who have not yet made a gift to the organization (for example non-giving alumni of a university), or the wider community. Some nonprofits opt to address this issue by purchasing or trading mailing lists.

- **Converting first-time donors into repeat donors:** New donor acquisition is expensive. It often costs nonprofits more money to get the first gift from a donor than that gift is worth. The second gift usually is the one that truly helps the organization, and is a good indicator that the donor may become a reliable donor for some time. Nonprofits need to take great care to ensure that a first time gift is renewed at some point in the near future. By the time a donor makes their third gift, they tend to be fairly loyal to the organization.
- **Leveraging reoccurring gifts:** If the organization can offer opportunities for donors to make regular, reoccurring gifts, take advantage of that as much as possible. Automatic monthly gifts by credit card, payroll deduction, or ACH withdrawal are an option, as are multi-year pledges for larger amounts.

As I mentioned at the beginning of this chapter, the Annual Fund is the foundation for long-term sustainability and success of the organization. Regular support leads to regular communication, engagement, and interaction with the organization, which over time builds appreciation, loyalty and trust. The donor knows at a very personal level that the work you do is meaningful and makes an impact. That creates a relationship between the donor and the nonprofit that opens up opportunities for larger gifts.

Stepping It Up: Major Gifts

For the long-term growth of any organization, significant philanthropic gifts are essential. Any successful major gift program will always start with individual donor prospects. It is almost always the case that major gifts are the result of a relationship that was initially established with a gift to the organization's Annual Fund. Rarely do major gifts appear "out of the blue" without some prior interaction between the nonprofit and the donor. The best way to illustrate this is the four-stage Giving Cycle.

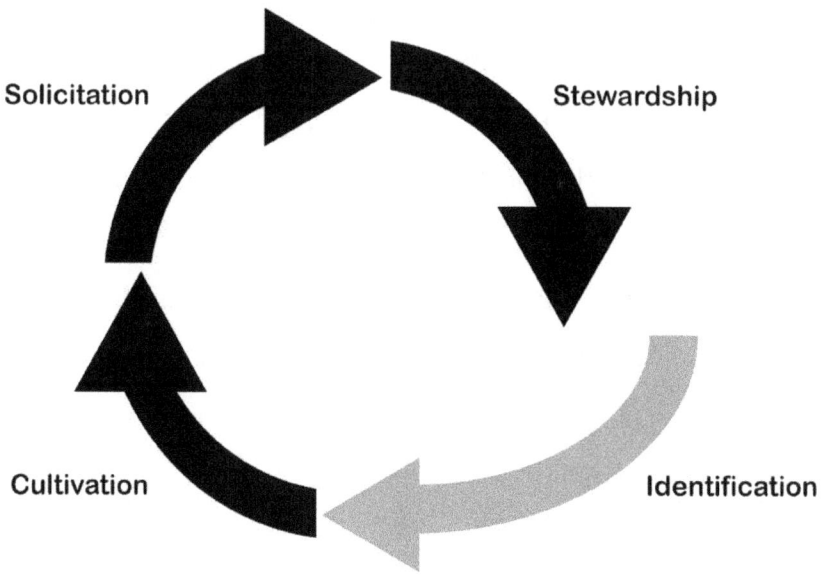

The first stage is donor **identification**. This can happen through self-identification (the donor makes a gift to the organization thereby making their interest known), or by identification through staff or volunteers before a gift is made ("Susan Smith likes to support causes like ours, and she just sold her business. We should invite her to our next event and get to know her better.").

The second stage is **cultivation**: the organization reaches out to the donor, and begins to engage them in a variety of ways, for example by sending them newsletters, inviting them to events, setting up a meeting with the Executive Director, offering a tour of the facility. The intent is to form a deeper relationship with the prospective donor through a series of progressive activities. We want to get to know them, understand what motivates and is important to them, and determine which aspect of our organization and programs appeals to them the most. This process of donor engagement and cultivation will help the organization determine what kind of gift amount to ask for. Alternatively, it can also help determine if the donor is not a good prospect to make a significant gift at this point in time. A determination of "not now" does not mean "not ever" as far as the potential for a large gift is concerned.

The third stage is the actual **solicitation** of the major gift. I will cover this in more detail in a moment. Any request for a large gift will be the result of careful planning, preparation, timing, and execution.

Assuming that the donor agrees to make a gift to the organization, the fourth stage begins: the **stewardship** of the donor and the gift. The organization makes sure that the gift is used according to the wishes of the donor, and reports back on outcomes and accomplishments that happened as a result of the donor's generosity. Proper stewardship of the funds and the donor are essential, because the best prospects for future gifts are donors who have made significant gifts to the organization in the past.

So how do you determine if a particular individual is a potential candidate for a major gift? The key to any major gift comes down to how well the donor is connected to the organization, their personal financial position, and their interest in the organization's mission and goals. I call it their **association**, their **ability**, and their **affinity**. As major gift fundraisers, we need to *confirm that all three conditions are present,* or the potential for a major gift is simply not there. Trying to force a major gift will only lead to wasted efforts and disappointment.

Let's take a closer look at each of the three required conditions. The **association** determines how closely the donor is connected to the organization. The closer the association, the stronger the link. The donor identification stage will help determine what that connection currently looks like, and subsequent cultivation efforts can help strengthen that link between donor and organization. A link can be very basic: does the donor know about the organization at all? Are they on our mailing list? Do they attend events? Are they friends with one of our volunteers? Do they or someone close to them benefit from the services our organization has to offer? Have they made a gift or do they volunteer for us?

The more of these connections with the donor exist, the greater the association to the organization. If there are none or only very few, the organization may need to work to strengthen the relationship first before a request for a major gift can be made.

While the organization has a fair amount of influence on how closely the donor is associated with the organization, the donor's financial **ability** to make a gift is an entirely different thing. This is where a carefully implemented, comprehensive fundraising program can be helpful. The donor may have assets that are underperforming, and a carefully structured charitable donation may be of significant value to them. A multi-year pledge may also be a way to allow the donor to structure a significant gift so it becomes a lot more manageable for them. Additionally, even if the donor is not in a position now to make a financial commitment, there is still a possibility to discuss leaving a part of their estate to the organization. I will discuss this further in the chapter on planned giving.

So how do you determine the right amount to ask for? The answer to that is driven by the needs of the organization, as well as the estimated capacity of the donor. If the organization needs a leadership gift for a specific project or campaign, it most likely has a very clear idea of what would constitute a "leadership gift" in that situation. In the case of a $10 million capital campaign, a leadership gift may be $2 million. If the donor has the capacity to make a gift of that amount, this should be the amount you ask for. On the other hand, if you are looking to raise money for a particular project and the estimated project cost is $20,000, ask for that amount – even if the donor has the ability to give more than that.

Determining a donor's wealth can be tricky. There are commercial wealth screening services available that compile a multitude of public records and information to develop wealth profiles of potential donors. These services are typically fairly expensive, but if the nonprofit is looking to embark on a capital campaign that will require securing many large gifts, it is an investment worth making. While not foolproof, the screening and assessment of potential donors can help set a baseline for expectations that will require further vetting and qualifying by volunteers and fundraising staff.

Once the donor has identified a list of potential major donors, conduct a series of confidential discussions with volunteers, board members, and staff to review each potential donor. Wealth screenings alone may not capture that the donor has children or grandchildren. They may not give any insight into the personal or professional situation of the donor. Are they taking care of nursing home expenses for an ailing relative? Is their oldest child about to start their degree at an expensive private college? Was the donor recently made partner at their firm? Have they sold or acquired real estate? A wealth screening may not necessarily pick up those details that other donors or volunteers close to the prospective donor may know.

The key is to get to know the potential donor, and develop a proposal for a gift the organization can justify asking for. What we don't want is "analysis paralysis" where staff and volunteers spend so much time talking, evaluating, reviewing, and planning that no one ever gets around to actually meeting with the prospective donor to ask for their gift.

The final condition is the donor's **affinity** for the organization and the cause. Our donor may have a long history of supporting children's causes: from pre-schools to afterschool programs, to coat and toy drives. Our organization might be focused on raising funds for research to help overcome childhood diseases. While children are still at the center of our efforts and clearly something the donor cares about, the donor may not be interested in contributing to medical research or other health-related causes. However, if the donor has made a gift to our Annual Fund, that's a strong indicator that interest is there. Likewise, if we can determine that the donor has given money to another organization with a mission similar to ours, this also indicates that there is an affinity for our cause.

One thing to keep in mind is that major gifts almost always require face-to-face asks. One individual will need to ask another individuals. It also matters *who* is asking for the gift. A major gift is most likely to occur if the right person is asking the right donor for the right amount, and at the right time.

The right person is ideally a peer who has already made their own gift. A peer can be a volunteer, a board member, or someone who knows the prospective donor personally and has a good relationship with them. It is critical that the person asking for a gift is intimately familiar with the organization, the campaign, and the project. It is also critical that this individual has already given or made a commitment of their own to have credibility. The personal commitment can also be used as a starting point for asking the other person for a gift, for example: "I have personally committed $10,000 to the organization, and I am asking you to consider a gift of $10,000 as well."

If there is no peer available to ask for a major gift, the Executive Director or a key member of the fundraising staff can fill that role. Often, a staff member of the organization and a committed volunteer visit a prospective donor together. The volunteer can make the case for the organization and why they opted to contribute themselves. The staff member can provide further insight and lend additional credibility. Some volunteers are also uncomfortable asking for a gift, but will help set-up a meeting, and be a spokesperson for the organization. The role of the staff member is then to ask the prospective donor for their support.

The right donor is hopefully one who has been identified, engaged, and properly prepared for this visit. It is important not to surprise the prospective donor with a request for a significant gift. The donor should be well aware of the fundraising effort of the organization (perhaps not in great detail, but there should be a general understanding of where the organization hopes to go).

When setting up the meeting, let the donor know that you would like to visit with them to talk about the campaign and how they could be involved. If the donor agrees to the meeting, it is already a fairly good sign that they are open to the idea of making a gift. Depending on the size of the donation requested, asking to meet with both the donor and their spouse or partner is highly advisable. It is preferred to visit with the donor at their home.

The right amount and the right time is hopefully something that previous conversations and engagement efforts have helped determine.

When making the request for a gift, it is important to be specific – both for what you are fundraising for, and also how much you want. Being unclear about what you want will only undermine the effort. Avoid phrasing the request along the lines of "helping with the campaign" or "consider making a contribution". It needs to be specific both in the gift amount well as what the organization will be using it for.

Especially for first-time fundraisers, this part of the process can be extremely anxiety inducing. It helps to rehearse in advance with another volunteer standing in for the prospective donor. If more than one person is going to be visiting the donor, discuss your plan first, and decide who will ask for the gift and when. Asking for the donation itself need to be short and direct. It may help you to modify this sentence for your own purposes, and then practice saying it: "I am hoping that you will join me in this effort for Good Hearts Animal Shelter, and make a gift of $20,000 to our kennel expansion campaign."

At that point, allow the potential donor (and their spouse or partner, if present) the opportunity to respond. Having provided all the necessary information, state your request, and then remain quiet. The donor may agree, decline, or have further questions, but it is important that **the donor be given the opportunity to break the silence and respond first**. If the donor agrees to make a gift, you can proceed to discuss the details (how the gift will be made, a timeline for potential installments, and finally complete a pledge card). If the donor declines, try to gain an understanding of their objections. Is the timing for a gift not right? Is the amount we asked for too high? Would the donor consider giving a smaller gift? Try to determine if the donor is telling you "no", or if it's a "not now". Thank the donor for their time and conclude your visit. If the donor has questions answer them, or schedule a follow-up call or visit if you first need to gather additional information.

Remember, not making a gift is not a rejection of the person asking for it. It just means that right now – whatever the reason may be – the donor is choosing not to donate to your cause. Keep them engaged and involved. The time may come when you can visit them again to present another opportunity to help support your cause.

Comprehensive Fundraising: Planned Giving

Planned giving is an important element of any comprehensive fundraising plan. Every nonprofit should at least consider encouraging donors to include the organization in their will.

What makes planned giving unique is the timing aspect of the gift: while the donor makes their commitment to the organization now (potentially with the option to change their mind later), the organization won't receive or benefit from the gift until sometime later, usually when the donor passes. Quite often, planned gifts are the largest gift a donor will make to an organization, and they can have a dramatic impact: in my first fundraising job, the institution I worked for ended up receiving an eight-figure gift from the estate of a local supporter. The gift came at a time when it wasn't entirely clear that we would make it through the fiscal year. That donor's generosity allowed us to keep the doors open, and brought some desperately needed stability to the organization.

As good of a story as this is, that gift was not an accident. It was the result of careful planning, and keeping the donor engaged over a long period of time without the benefit of an immediate payout. Planned giving requires strategic patience from the organization, and a willingness to invest time and resources into donors with only the possibility of a gift at a much later date.

In this case, the gift was a fairly straightforward commitment the donor made by including our organization in their will. It is also the easiest type of planned gift to promote and process. There are numerous other ways of structuring deferred gifts: for example gift annuities, charitable remainder annuity trusts and unitrusts, gifts through individual retirement accounts and donor advised funds. All of them are more complex to implement, and in some cases require additional fees, operational reserves, and legal filings. These efforts may be worthwhile and should be carefully considered. For the purpose of this book, I will limit planned giving to simple bequests which can be incorporated into the fundraising program of every organization. The other should be discussed by the board of directors, ideally in consultation with a planned giving expert or financial advisor. It may also be beneficial to reach out to any local community foundations to see if they offer programs that allow the community foundation to administer certain programs on behalf of the organization. This potentially allows the nonprofit to offer a wider range of giving vehicles without needing to incur administrative and financial liabilities.

Even with a comparatively simple planned giving program that focuses exclusively on bequests, it can be helpful for the organization to consult with a financial planning professional or estate attorney. These professionals may be able to advise the organization during the process of creating marketing collateral and informational materials for donors. In addition, knowing more about your organization may make that attorney or financial advisor a potential resource for donors looking to support specific nonprofits with their estate. Sometimes, donors write their will with a specific cause in mind without knowing which organizations in their community already address those needs. An advisor, who is intimately familiar with your organization and your work, may be able to foster those connections.

To implement a planned giving program, the organization will need buy-in from their board of directors, a gift acceptance policy, and promotional materials for donors. The most important piece should be sample language for making a bequest that donors can incorporate into their will, or add to their written will in the form of a codicil. The key elements that should be included are:

- **General statement of intent:** "I [Name of Donor] hereby give, devise, and bequeath…"
- **Identification of the recipient organization:** "…to [Name of Organization] a 501(c)(3) nonprofit organization [tax ID number], in [City, State]…". *Note: including the tax ID number is not necessarily a requirement, but can be extremely helpful – especially with smaller organizations or organizations that have names that may make it easy to mistake them with another, similarly named organization.*
- **Purpose:** "…for the use of [General operations or specific program or purpose]…" *Note: ideally, the purpose is made clear in consultation with the donor. If the program is already established, this part is easy. If the donor wants to use their estate gift to establish a brand new program, additional discussions may need to take place in advance, and additional gift documentation may need to be put into place.*
- **Amount:** "…the sum of [$_____] OR [__%] percent of all the rest, residue, and remainder of my estate]." *Note: if the donor specifies an amount, the organization can record the gift accordingly. If the donor specifies a percentage of the estate, it helps for internal planning purposes to ask the donor for a general good-faith estimate how much that percentage might represent in actual dollars. The donor may opt not to disclose that information, which is perfectly valid.*

Including an organization in their will affords donors the opportunity to hold on to their assets and feel good about supporting a cause important to them without worrying about potentially giving up on life savings that they may need in their retirement. A will also allows donors to change their mind in the future. They can choose to name a different organization, add additional beneficiaries, or change intended gift amounts. The value for the nonprofit is that donors typically do not write organizations out of their will once they have been added in. It can, however, happen that donors, upon reviewing their will, increase their designated charitable giving amount.

With all these pieces in place, all that's left is promoting planned giving to donors and supporters of the organization. Annual Fund reply cards and online donation forms should be updated to include a checkbox or a byline with a sentence along the lines of "Please contact me about leaving [name of organization] in my will." If the organization has a regular newsletter or Facebook page, it helps to occasionally feature a donor who has included the organization in their will. In addition to publishing an annual Honor Roll of Donor, the organization should also publish any non-anonymous donors who have included the organization in their estate plans.

Corporate Gifts: What's In It for Them?

In 2014, Standard & Poor's released a report showing that the top 18 wealthiest companies in the U.S. held over a third of all the wealth in the country.

When seeking financial support for your cause, it can be tempting to look to corporations for the quick fix to your fundraising needs. After all, as the thinking goes, companies make a lot of money and thus have a lot of money to give away. Research done by the Lilly Family School of Philanthropy at Indianapolis University shows that corporate donations to nonprofits year after year only make up around 5% of all charitable giving. In addition, the percentage of corporate pre-tax profits that are made as charitable contributions is barely at a 1%.

The main reason is simple: companies are about making money, not giving it away. Some businesses even embrace the notion that creating value and profits for their shareholders is their way of giving back to the community. A small number of corporations believe in the idea that being philanthropic is a form of investing in their own future, by that number is very small.

It wasn't until 1953 when a legal decision in favor of A.P. Smith Manufacturing Company made it clear that corporations were within their rights to give a portion of their profits away as charitable gifts. The directors of the company had approved a gift of $1,500 to Princeton University. A group of shareholders sued, claiming that the company had improperly given away profits that the shareholders were entitled to. A New Jersey court decided that as long as making charitable donations did not result in any conflicts of interest for the directors, the corporation had every right to be philanthropic.

This legal battle underlined that being charitable is just not part of the DNA of corporations in our society, and that activities that don't contribute to overall profits can land them in a difficult spot.

Of course, there are exceptions. A family-owned, private corporation will likely act differently than a publically traded Fortune 500 company. A strong personal connection between someone on the nonprofit board with someone at the leadership level of a company can be a tremendous asset. The community bank whose CEO serves on your board represents a far better possibility for a corporate gift than another bank in town that has no ties to your organization whatsoever.

Unlike individuals, who may have a multitude of possible reasons for supporting you, in the case of corporations it is much more direct: **What is in it for them?**

- Does your organization directly serve individuals that are a primary consumer market for the company?
- Do you represent a market they want to have a greater presence in?
- Does supporting your cause enhance their brand or promote their products to an audience that is relevant to them?
- Are you able to capture who our organization is reaching, and to what extent that might result in positive exposure for the company?

This may sounds suspiciously like advertising and sponsorship, and that is because in many ways it is. Some CEOs and corporate leaders believe that giving back to the community is a good thing, but the driver behind it is almost always that a thriving community is in some way also good for the company. People in the community might be more inclined to give their business to the business that gives back to them. A company may also think that a vibrant community might lead to greater employee satisfaction. Corporations will consider charitable contributions if they believe that there are short or long-term benefits in it for them. As a fundraiser, it is your job to make a proposal that captures those tangible and intangible benefits. You need to make the case that supporting your organization is good for them.

Some companies have started to integrate corporate social responsibility programs into their business plan, and as a result have begun to formalize much of their charitable giving. If you are looking to engage a business in a philanthropic partnership, research their funding guidelines and priorities. Whatever your proposal and donor recognition package ends up being, make sure it aligns with the company's stated goals.

For a nonprofit, this can be a fine line to walk. Corporate benefactors deserve credit for their generosity, but too much credit and too much promotion of the gift may veer into a territory where it's closer to advertising than philanthropy. If the benefit becomes more tangible than mere recognition (for example, Company A supports the community theater company by purchasing a full page of advertising in the playbill for $3,000; Company B makes a $2,500 gift to the theater company, and in return is giving a full page in the program thanking them for their donation), it might fall in the category of Unrelated Business Income (UBIT), and potentially become taxable. In addition, the corporation may not be able to claim a tax credit for the full amount of their donation. Spelling out donor recognition practices in advance can be valuable in this situation. When in doubt, the nonprofit might want to seek out the advice of a professional familiar with nonprofit laws and UBITs to review their corporate benefactor program.

More importantly, corporate support at levels that result in significant donor recognition will automatically tie the organization to the brand of the company. Corporations are very conscientious of their brand and who they partner with. Nonprofits should feel empowered to be equally aware and just as protective of their brand. Before accepting a large corporate gift or entering into a partnership agreement, consider how the association with that business will reflect on your organization. A recreational soccer league partnering with a sporting goods store is probably a great fit. A local health clinic receiving funding from a tobacco company may raise some concerns.

Be mindful that corporate contributions add more to the organization than just cash. It should be viewed as an equal partnership. As such the nonprofit needs to be mindful of how that partnership will be seen in their community and among their supporters. It can be a good thing, but the wrong partnership it can also become a public relations headache. Always keep in mind that a large corporate gift includes both:

the cash, and the association of your organization with the corporate funder.

Grant Writing: Foundations Have the Money?

Like corporations, foundations also approach any requests for funding with an eye toward cost-benefit analysis. Corporations will make a donation with some consideration for a return on their investment. Foundations will evaluate proposals by determining which ones best advance their own mission. In the ideal scenario, the mission of the foundation and the nonprofit overlap, and the grant making process becomes a partnership rather than a contractual obligation.

In order for a nonprofit to be successful with their grant application, it is imperative that their funding need is in alignment with the funding objectives of the foundation. Research carefully what the foundation will and will not fund. If your mission, program focus, or geographic area is specifically excluded in the funding guidelines, do not apply. Assuming there is overlap between your needs and the foundation's funding priorities, you are ready to proceed.

The next step is to look closely at the recommended process for submitting a request for funding. The majority of foundations have websites that spell out the requirements in detail, including staff members in charge of evaluating funding requests for specific programmatic areas. Follow these guidelines *exactly*. If the foundation asks for a single page proposal, only send one single page. If the foundation asks for a budget, include one. If it is requested to provide a listing of staff members involved with the project, provide it. If they don't want your application stapled, do not staple the pages. Don't include information that isn't specifically requested. If the foundation requires an initial letter of inquiry, send that and wait for a formal invitation. Adhere to all deadlines. Foundations are flooded with requests for funding, and if a request can be rejected on a technicality, it will be. Grant makers only have a limited amount of time to review proposals, and only a limited pool of funding that can be given out during their funding year. The quicker the applicant pool can be narrowed down, the better it is for them. It is not uncommon for national foundations to receive hundreds of proposal a day, and very often their staffing levels are minimal for the amount of funding requests they have to review.

Most grant makers do not have the time to take calls from first-time grant requestors. If a grantor is accepting unsolicited proposals, the information is usually shared on their website along with any requirements for the initial letter of inquiry. If there aren't any, a typical letter of inquiry will include the following elements:

- **Introduction:** An executive summary that includes the name of your organization, reference to your 501(c)(3) tax exempt status, the amount requested for the project, and a brief description of what you are looking to accomplish. Include key project leaders, a brief description how you are planning to measure and evaluate outcomes, and a general project timeline (when you would start, key milestones, when the project is expected to conclude).
- **Organization description:** A very concise summary of the mission and activities of the organization, current programs directly related to the request (ideally information on any pilot programs that have shown initial success), and why your organization is uniquely suited to successfully carry out the project.
- **Statement of need:** Why is this project important enough to deserve consideration for funding? Who will be served by this project, and how? Is there specific data available to illustrate the need, and is there any evidence that a project like the one you are proposing has shown success in addressing those needs?
- **The methodology:** The methodology summarizes how the project will address the need outlined in the needs statement

above. It will also outline how the effectiveness of the project will be measured and assessed, and what data points you intend to capture. This part in particular must be developed in close collaboration with the individual running the program. If there is a data tracking component, they must know about it and have input upfront.

- **Other funding sources:** Explain briefly if other funding partners are involved, and if the organization is contributing some of their own financial resources to make the project a success. If the organization intends for the project to become self-sustaining after the grant money runs out, explain how you plan to achieve that outcome.
- **Executive summary:** Restate once more the need and the intent of your organization, and who the funder should contact for additional questions.

When writing a letter of inquiry, look over the foundation's website for specific keywords and priorities. Even if your mission already aligns closely with the foundation's objectives, it is still extremely important to use the terminology, keywords, and phrases the grant maker uses. Especially large grant makers at times rely on automated submission systems that will flag applications based on keywords (or lack thereof). The greater the number of matching keywords, the better the chance that the letter of inquiry will get advanced to the next stage of the review process.

At that point, how the organization will measure the impact and outcomes will play a crucial role. Grant makers only have a limited pool of funding and look to maximize it as best as they can. It is your job as the grant application writer to help the funder understand how their money will be used, and how many people will be impacted by the grant. The way grants are made at some foundations is that grant officers will evaluate and then select their favorites from the total number of grant applications that came in. At the appropriate board meeting, the grant officer will advocate for funding on behalf of the grants that they feel will be the most impactful and most effective. The board usually acts on the recommendation of the grant officer, provided there is sufficient funding available. It is the fundraiser's responsibility to provide enough data, examples, and analysis so the grant officer at the foundation can effectively present the case. Of course it never hurts if the grant application is exciting to read but the two aspects that ultimately will weigh in the most are alignment with the goals and objectives of the grant maker, and a clear description how and why this particular project will have an impact.

Most grant proposal writers have an approximate success rate of about 10% (in other words, grant making organizations fund about 1 out of every 10 grant applications). Grant funding should absolutely be in the conversation of every comprehensive fundraising program, but be mindful that good proposals take time to develop and that outcome isn't guaranteed. Some nonprofits choose to specifically invest in the position of a grant proposal writer, knowing that investing in the development of several proposals a year will pay off in the long run.

Government Grants

If you thought corporate and foundation funding was challenging to come by, then government grants are really not for the faint of heart. If you abhor paperwork, then government grants are not for you. Granted, some towns and municipalities sometimes provide funding for nonprofits, which can be a more accessible and involve a far less cumbersome process. While those are technically also government grants, in this section I am writing about state and federal grants.

Because funding for these types of grants comes from tax dollars, proposal budgets are heavily scrutinized. Individuals, corporations, and foundations are often satisfied with succinct updates and a minimal outcomes report. However, if you choose to pursue government funding, be fully prepared that the paperwork, record keeping, and reporting requirements throughout and especially at the conclusion of the project are immense. Every penny must be accounted for, and it must be spent exactly as the original budget outlined. If you find yourself running short on marketing dollars or salaries midway through the project, that is your problem to solve. You cannot shift funds from one line item to another to make up a shortfall. If you run short on cash overall or in a specific line item, your organization must make up the difference. Careful planning prior to submitting a proposal is absolutely essential.

Record keeping and reporting for government grants can be extremely time consuming and overwhelming. If you think you are going to be operating at capacity just to deliver services, then government grants may not be the right thing for your organization. The administrative burden may be too much to take on.

Government grants can be great, but as an organization you need to approach them with a complete and clear-eyed understanding of everything that is entailed. Your organization's leaders, your board, and your staff need to be on board.

It pays to find out which government agency at the federal or state level is most likely to issue requests for proposals that fit your mission, and then monitor their website and news feeds. Some government grant announcements are made with a very long lead time. Others give potential applicants only a very short window to apply. It helps to always have conversations about potential funding opportunities internally so that when the time comes, the person writing the grant proposal has all the information they need already in hand.

A Word on Capital Campaigns

Capital campaigns are the pinnacle of fundraising. There is an enormous amount of complexity and preparation involved with conducting a successful capital campaign, and it should not be taken lightly. I wrote this book with the intention to provide a solid foundation of the principles and practices of fundraising. With regard to capital campaigns, I will provide a general overview and highlight things to be mindful of in the planning process. However, in this particular case it may be best to consult with an experienced fundraising professional or fundraising consulting firm.

Before embarking on any form of capital campaign, it pays to have a well-maintained donor database and study it carefully. How many donors does your organization consider to be major donors? For some organizations, a major gift is $1,000. For others it's $5,000, and a few select nonprofits don't even begin major donor stewardship efforts until the gift commitment reaches $10,000. Aside from major gifts, how many donors have given three years, five years, or even ten years in a row? What are the average gift amounts your organization receives? How many donors have a cumulative life-time giving total of $1,000, $10,000, or $20,000? How many individuals who have ever given to the organization are in the database with good contact information? All of these are key data points that will help determine if the stated goal of your capital campaign is even a possibility.

While it may be the case that a high-profile capital campaign could attract new potential donors, this is a strategy fraught with risks. Typically, a major gift is not the first gift a donor will make to an organization, and generally past major gift donors are the best prospective donors for future major gifts. Yes, it is possible to achieve a capital campaign goal by bringing in numerous new major donors, but it will be absolutely critical to work with a network of dedicated fundraising volunteers. The organization on its own won't be able to achieve its goal if a large number of as-of-yet unaffiliated major gift prospects are required.

After assessing the internal donor pool, it often pays to perform a wealth screening on the entire database of current and potential donors. There are numerous professional wealth screening services available. The website of the Association of Prospect Researcher for Advancement (www.aprahome.org) or the Association of Fundraising Professionals (www.afpnet.org) will have a list of companies that offer the services you are looking for. Those services are not cheap and are not entirely without flaws, but they will be an essential tool to ensure that your campaign targets the right prospects at the right time. Let me reiterate: these services are not cheap, both in terms of their fee structure but also in terms of the organization's staff time. Pulling the data for the donor wealth analysis is time consuming, and getting the research data back into the system can be equally time consuming. Capital campaigns are one of those cases where the saying "you need to spend money to make money" holds absolutely true. The lead-up cost to a successful capital campaign can be quite substantial, especially for smaller nonprofits with an already tight budget. If this is the case for your organization, it may be worthwhile to seek a capacity building foundation grant first before fully committing to the rigors and expenses of a capital campaign.

The next phase of the capital campaign planning phase is a feasibility study. Select a handful of donors and community members (about two to three dozen), and ask them questions about the organization and the campaign.

- What do they think of the mission of the organization?
- Do they believe the organization serves an important need in the community?
- Are they aware of the services the organization provides and the people in the community it serves?

- How do they feel about the need for the proposed campaign?
- How do they feel about the amount of funding the organization is trying to raise?
- Do they have any questions or concerns about the project, the finances, or the leadership of the organization?
- Are there other capital campaigns currently happening in the community that might make it more difficult for this organization to successfully raise the required funds?
- Would they consider supporting the campaign (note: this is *not* a solicitation visit, and will not be followed-up with a request for a gift during this meeting)?
- Are there other individuals the person interviewed would suggest to the organization to speak with about the campaign?

A feasibility study is an ideal activity to engage an independent consulting firm, because interviewees may be more inclined to give frank and honest answers to a third party than they would if the Executive Director, a board member, or other respected community leader would be sitting in front of them. The consultant will then compile the responses and share them with the Executive Director, the board of directors, and other internal stakeholders. Any potential objections and concerns should be honestly and openly discussed. If the preliminary assessment reveals that it may be a challenge to raise significant gifts at the higher giving levels, the overall goal or the timeline for the campaign should be re-evaluated.

If all the initial planning steps indicate that the timing, the time table, and the overall goal for the capital campaign are on track, the next step is to establish a campaign steering committee. The campaign steering committee will be a mix of campaign volunteers, board members, and executive staff of the organization. Key positions of the campaign steering committee should be filled by volunteers with the ability and capacity to make major gifts who also have the connections to other high net worth individuals. In addition to a campaign chair (and possibly a campaign co-chair), the steering committee needs to appoint committee chairs for the various giving segments (for example gifts of $100,000 and up, gifts of $50,000 and up, gifts of $10,000 and up, etc.), committee chairs for any special events done in the context of the campaign, and finally a communications chair.

The role of the communications chair will be to help oversee the development of the communications plan and communication materials for the campaign. We have covered this in an earlier chapter with regard to the overall mission of the organization, but now the process needs to have a very specific focus on the campaign, the reason for the campaign, and potential questions, concerns, and objections. All of these discussions will lead to the development of campaign collaterals (brochures, website, etc.) and inform training materials and workshop content for volunteer fundraisers.

With the steering committee in place and the collateral and communication pieces developed, the role of the steering committee shifts to volunteer recruitment and volunteer training. The volunteer training itself will focus on a review of the campaign case, the communication pieces on hand, and practice runs of one-on-one gift solicitations. Volunteers will also be asked to make their own commitment to the campaign. Another component of the volunteer training is a review of prospective donors to identify potential relationships and match the right volunteer with the right person to request a gift. Each volunteer should be asked to only meet with about five potential donors. Any more than that, and you run the risk of overcommitting volunteers.

All of this work is typically done well in advance of any public announcement of the capital campaign. In addition, capital campaigns generally don't go public until about 50% of the goal has been raised or secured through firm commitments.

Some additional guidelines to assist with the planning of a capital campaign are:

- The lead gift will generally be between 15% and 25% of the goal.
- About 80% of the overall campaign goal will come from 20% of all donors.
- For each gift, your organization needs to identify three to five potential donors. In this case, potential or "qualified" donors means they have been identified through the database, the wealth screening process, and confirmed with fundraising campaign volunteers. Unless they have a relationship with you, Bill Gates, Warren Buffett, and Oprah Winfrey do not belong on this list.
- The campaign will need to identify more donors at the upper giving levels. As you work down the list, fewer prospects are needed because some people who declined to make a gift at the higher level may end up committing to smaller gifts at lower giving tiers.

While some organizations, especially large universities, are now in the mode of transitioning from one capital campaign to the next without much of a break in between, for smaller nonprofits a capital campaign may only happen once every ten years or even longer. Capital campaigns have the potential to significantly advance the mission of an organization, but they only succeed if mission, message, and strategic plan are in absolute alignment. The more an organization invests in the early planning stages, the greater the possibility of success for its capital campaign.

The People Who Make it all Work

Working With Your Board

Volunteers can be vital contributors to the success of your mission. Out of all your volunteers, your board of directors can be both your biggest asset and your biggest liability. Volunteers need to be paid attention to and be engaged in order to feel invested in the organization. That is especially true for leadership volunteers like board members. An invested volunteer can move mountains, particularly in fundraising.

Engaging the Board beyond Quarterly Meetings

An engaged and well-managed board of directors can be an extremely valuable asset for the organization. Individuals who agree to serve on the board of a nonprofit typically do so because they want to help and make a difference. While some will be limited to just the time it takes to participate in board meetings, others are eager to further lend their skills and experience to the organization. To get the most out of your board, know what prompted each board member to decide to get involved in the first place. Some may have a strong interest in a specific facet of the organization. Try to engage those board members through additional volunteer opportunities that directly connect with their interest and passion.

It helps to regularly assess the make-up of the board, and determine if there are any deficiencies. Deficiencies can be in the areas of diversity, skillsets, connections, and possibly wealth. If regularly reaching out to the community is a priority for the organization, are there individuals on the board of directors who have a background in marketing, communication, media relations, or social media? If the organization wants to make an effort to grow its planned giving program, is there someone on the board who has a legal background or is a financial planner and able to offer professional expertise? If the organization is dedicated to helping a particular group of individuals and families in the community, are there board members who represent that demographic or can speak knowledgeably on their behalf?

For all those reasons it can be helpful to have a standing membership recruitment committee, or convene it as an ad-hoc committee in regular intervals. Allow the committee to assess if the composition of the board still serves the organization, or if specific roles on the board need to be filled. It may help to develop a rubric of desired skills and traits to fill any vacancies more strategically. A recruitment committee can also provide valuable feedback on existing board communication and training materials. Especially when recruiting and onboarding new board members, asking current board members about their onboarding experience can be very helpful. In one of my past positions, one board member told me that she really appreciated seeing an organizational chart, a bio of the executive director, and bios of other board members in the recruitment package. All of those were pieces we had not paid too much attention to, but we made them a priority going forward.

Another subcommittee or ad-hoc committee worth considering is a communications committee. The role of the communications committee is to periodically assess the messaging and communication pieces of the organization, and provide feedback. This will be especially relevant in the lead-up to a capital campaign or an event of importance to the organization, like an anniversary celebration.

While most boards have a finance committee, I would argue that a component of the finance committee should be fundraising. If the board is large enough and has a sufficient number of volunteers, a separate fundraising committee may be possible and preferable. The role of the fundraising committee is to assist staff with fundraising and donor recognition activities, help recruit fundraising volunteers, and assist with arranging or participating in donor visits as needed. They may also periodically evaluate fundraising progress overall, and make recommendations regarding the number of fundraising staff employed by the organization.

Board members who feel they have a lot to offer can feel underutilized and undervalued if there are no other opportunities for them to serve the organization outside of regularly scheduled board meetings. For the staff, the key is to find a balance where those talents by the board can be effectively leveraged without creating "busy work". Ultimately, the staff needs to manage the board. In return, the board should provide strategic direction for the organization without micro-managing daily activities.

Your Board as a Fundraising Force

In the most ideal of circumstances, a board of directors is a highly engaged group of major donors, and a willing team of fundraisers who are very familiar with the goals and needs of the organization. For most boards, this will not be the case. You may never be able to convince every last board member to fundraise for the organization. That's perfectly fine. There are a number of others things board members can do that support the overall fundraising effort. There are also some things that staff members can do to better prepare hesitant board members for a more active role.

The first step of any fundraising effort is an assessment of needs. Since boards are tasked with ensuring the fiscal stability of the organization, discussing strategic initiatives and conducting a feasibility and cost analysis is something every board member should be able to take part in. Once a board agrees that funds need to be raised to achieve a certain goal, the foundation for further engagement is established.

The next step is developing the case for support and determining how to communicate that need to the right audience. Both of these steps are critically important to any successful fundraising drive. Note that as of yet no board member has been asked to visit with a potential donor and ask for a gift. Nonetheless, your board is already deeply involved in the fundraising process.

Now that we have completed the business plan and the marketing plan for our fundraising initiative, we can move on to the third step. This steps involves reviewing lists of potential prospects: those who the organization knows, and others the organization wants to involve at some point during the course of the fundraising initiative. Board members may have a good understanding of who the "movers and shakers" in the community are, and may be able to play a big role in helping the fundraising staff prioritize and rank potential prospects.

Board members can be an invaluable resource when it comes to determining the most appropriate ask amount for specific prospects.

This sets the stage for the next and very important step: after securing a gift from the chair of the board and the executive director, the chair and the executive director of the organization should meet with each board member individually and ask them personally for a gift to the cause. The expectations is that each board member would make a "leadership gift", however what that amount is can vary drastically. Two aspects should be emphasized: one, every board member needs to make some kind of financial commitment to the project, and two, the commitment needs to be above and beyond their typical annual gift.

Depending on the overall fundraising goal, additional volunteers may be needed. The fifth step would be a request to board members to help the organization recruit volunteer fundraisers. In most major gift initiatives, a volunteer would be asked to visit about three to five potential donors who they have a good relationship with. As most major gifts require about three to five leads (meaning a fundraiser may get turned down by four people before finally hearing a "Yes!" from the fifth potential donor on the list), this should give the fundraising staff and the board a sense of how many additional volunteers may need to be brought on board.

At this point, the members of the board have already been deeply involved in the conceptualization, planning, and execution of the fundraising plan. To move forward, formal major gift training may be required. Major gift training typically emphasizes roleplay, a review of the talking points, and specific conversations regarding which volunteer should reach out to which potential donor.

If a board member is still hesitant about wanting to be a fundraiser, the opportunity is there to address their questions and concerns as part of the formal volunteer training process. If they still feel uncomfortable with the idea of asking for support for the mission of the organization, that's fine. At this point, we have given them all the tools to be successful. Taking that final step is up to them. A reluctant fundraiser for the organization can potentially do more harm than good. It is important to keep in mind that any board member who has been actively engaged during steps one through five has already done a great service to the overall fundraising effort.

A Word about Board Insurance

Also referred to as Directors and Officers Liability Insurance, board insurance is a worthwhile expense to consider.

According to the Nonprofits Insurance Alliance Group (also a 501(c)(3) nonprofit organization), about 1 out of 100 nonprofits will file a claim each year with an average settlement amount of $28,000. The D&O Liability Insurance is meant to safeguard the nonprofit against claims of willful misconduct on the part of the board or the staff. While each nonprofit will have to evaluate for themselves if this is an investment worth making, I do encourage volunteer board members to ask if an organization has D&O Liability Insurance before committing to serve on their board of directors. Because the board is ultimately responsible for the sound fiscal management and operation of the nonprofit they oversee, a significant claim against the organization could potentially result in a personal liability claim against an individual board member. For example, if the nonprofit with approval from its board of directors signs a multi-year lease for their new facility but fails to make payments, the owner of the property may try to recoup the losses from the personal assets of board members.

While I don't want to discourage anyone from taking on a leadership role with a nonprofit, I do recommend asking a lot of questions before making the commitment to serve in that kind of capacity. Ask for a copy of the balance sheet. Study the profit and loss statement. Inquire about assets, income projections, and anticipated expenses. Does the organization have a written list of responsibilities and expectations for members of their board? Ask about board insurance. If a nonprofit does not carry D&O Liability Insurance, that does not mean you should automatically turn down their request serve on their board, but it's best to make the commitment with a full understanding of what risks and responsibilities you might be taking on.

Serving on the board of a nonprofit can be fun and fulfilling. The experience will be far more rewarding if you can make that commitment with an understanding of what your expectations are of the organization, and what the organization expects of you.

Working with Volunteers

Volunteers are often able to pitch in and lend extra support to an organization, but effective volunteer management requires careful planning and proper support. Organizations that rely heavily on volunteers to deliver services often have one or more dedicated staff members managing them, providing volunteer training and orientation programs.

Before engaging volunteers, it is helpful to develop job descriptions and explicitly spell out their responsibilities and your expectations. Some organizations go as far as having volunteers sign a letter of agreement, and provide job review and feedback. All of those steps will allow the organization to provide high-impact and meaningful volunteer opportunities. Don't forget to develop a proper recognition program for your volunteers as well.

In the ideal scenario, volunteers can offer time and expertize in a way that contributes significantly to the organization's bottom line. The Independent Sector, a leadership network of nonprofits, foundations, and corporations, has estimated the value of a volunteer hour at $23.56 for 2015 (the most recent year available at the writing of this chapter). That number is comprised of a general salary combined with payroll taxes and fringe benefits that the organization might otherwise have had to allocate to a paid staff member. For organizations like Doctors Without Borders, the donated skilled labor is clearly even more value.

As an exercise, I encourage you to track the amount of volunteer hours donated to your organization each year, and multiply that number by $23.56. Used correctly, volunteers can have a very significant impact on your budget, which in turn lets you direct potential savings to other aspects of your operations. In addition, for younger supporters a volunteer opportunity is frequently the first connection they make with your organization. That connection then becomes a stepping stone to future financial support.

If you have a volunteer who absolutely loves fundraising, let them help you reach out to donors. Other volunteers can still play an important role in your organization's fundraising program:

- They can serve as a focus group for your case for support.
- Some volunteers can be a helpful market check: is your organization expanding its corporate sponsorship program? Get input from volunteers in leadership and management positions at local companies.
- Have volunteers give input on prospective donors.

- Ask volunteers to help make introductions to individuals the organization would like to connect with.
- Have volunteers engaged in recruitment, event promotion, and marketing efforts.
- Could volunteers support communication efforts by writing press releases or newsletters? Could they help with photos and posts on social media?

Volunteers can be a significant asset. It takes commitment by the organization, but those who engage and manage their volunteers in a thoughtful manner can benefit tremendously.

Special Events

Some of my colleagues in the fundraising profession stand by two unshakeable beliefs: newsletters and special events are a waste of time and resources, and the practice of both needs to be ended. Let's save the discussion about newsletters for the upcoming chapter on marketing and focus on special events for now. In principle, there are two kinds of special events an organization might work on: one aimed at raising funds, the other an investment by the organization in current and future donor relations.

Special events put on for the sake of raising funds can be challenging to evaluate. Organizations often simply take event revenue and subtract hard expenses (facility rental, catering fee, invitation design, printing, and postage). The result – while a starting point – does not necessarily represent the actual net gain for the organization. To properly assess costs, staff time and volunteer hours should be factored in. If a special event consumes so much of the organization's lead fundraiser's time that major donor visits and gift proposals are significantly compromised, the administration and implementation of the event may need to be revisited.

Another potential downside is an "all eggs in one basket" approach to special events. Some smaller organizations build a lion share of their annual revenue around the success of one major gala, silent auction, or annual golf outing. If for some reason the event is poorly attended, a major sponsor falls through, or the weather doesn't play along, the operating budget for the year could be in serious jeopardy. If an organization chooses to remain invested in special event fundraisers, it also needs to be prepared to diversify its founding sources as best as it can.

Still, there is one major aspect to special events, which is why organizations often find it difficult to let go of them completely: all organizations worry about donor attrition and overextending their current volunteers. Every year, it is inevitable that some donors will not renew their support and that some volunteers will find other (and perhaps more rewarding) ways to spend their time. That's not the fault of the organization or an unpredictability from their supporter, it is just the natural life cycle. Organizations *have* to reach out to new potential supporters *constantly*, and need to have a plan for doing so. Some organizations will buy mailing lists to bolster their Annual Fund. Others may rely heavily on their board and volunteers to bring in new prospects. Many count on events to expose new people to the organization and bring them into the fold.

If the purpose of your organization's special events is to attract new volunteers and supporters, a cohesive strategy must be built around that objective.

- Is the organization effectively promoting the event to new audiences?
- Are board members, staff, and volunteers helping get the word out?
- Is there a budget dedicated to outreach and promotion? Is the effectiveness of the outreach effort being measured in any way and adjusted year to year?
- Is there a mechanism in place leading up to and during the event to capture contact information of attendees?
- Is there a follow-up activity after the event is done?
- Is there a strategy in place to convert donors into volunteers, and volunteers into donors over the following weeks and months?

If those elements are in place, the investment of time and money into special events may very well be worth the effort. It will pay off in the long run to look beyond just donor recognition and funds raised when evaluating events.

Lastly, there is one more aspect to special events that should not be overlooked. The majority of special events are still focused on reunions, silent auctions, galas, golf outings, and the like. They tend to be aimed at older, more established donors, and for years have done so very well. Organizations can no longer overlook the reality that the Baby Boomer generation is getting older. Their ability to financially and physically participate in fundraising events as they have in the past is diminishing. As nonprofits, we need to make sure that a continued investment in special events also involves younger generations. Millennials in particular aren't necessarily in a position yet to support charities in a significant way, but will give generously of their time and their skills. Many Millennials view a contribution of their time equally valuable to a contribution of cash. For many Millennials participation in an event is their first connection point with a nonprofit, while for Boomers the first point of contact is often their first gift (and it usually comes through a mail appeal).

Nonprofits need to be aware that as donor and volunteer demographics are shifting, so should our approaches to outreach and engagement. The kinds of special events that worked well ten years ago may need to be re-conceptualized for shifts in our target audience.

Generational Fundraising

For fundraising purposes, the three most significant generations are Boomers (born after World War II and through 1964), Gen-Xers (born between 1965 and 1984), and Millennials (born between 1985 and 2004). Before we dive into what distinguishes them, let's first discuss what is consistent among these generations across the board.

Being clear in what your organization does, who it serves, and how it tries to accomplish its goals needs to be clear in all your messaging – regardless of who you talk to. Older donors may continue giving out of a sense of loyalty, but even they will not be motivated to make a major gift unless your mission and purpose is clearly defined, and your vision and values is in alignment with their own values.

That said, there are a few distinctions that may require you to modify your approach and your message. Please note that these are meant to offer only a strategic roadmap for planning donor engagement. The best major fundraising programs find ways to tailor their messages to each individual gift prospect.

Baby Boomers tend to favor traditional institutions: their churches, their university, etc. They tend to respond to mail appeals better than any of the other generations, and are least comfortable with online giving, or fundraising through social media. Their involvement tends to be primarily as financial contributors, but do not underestimate their volunteer potential if the right opportunity is presented. Donors of this generation should definitely be on your radar for planned gifts. They can be extremely valuable as members on your board, but can also at times express that their social connections for major gift work "are not what they used to be".

Gen-Xers tend to stay away from traditional institutions and look for nonprofits they believe will make a significant impact in the areas they feel most strongly about. While loyalty was a key factor for Boomers, Gen-Xers will give to "traditional" institutions as long as they believe those institutions are innovating and changing lives. Boomers give because they have faith in the organization, Gen-Xers give if the organization can demonstrate that their faith in the institution is justified. Organizations need to prove themselves before the Gen-Xer will make an investment. On the other hand, Gen-Xers also tend to go "all-in", meaning once an organization has earned their trust and support, Gen-Xers will look for other opportunities to further their cause. This generation is primed for leadership roles on your board and on key fundraising and program initiatives. In addition to major gifts, Gen-Xers should also not be overlooked at potential planned giving prospects.

Gen-Xers are very comfortable with online giving and are savvy donors. Your website must absolutely be equipped to handle online contributions. Gen-Xers will respond to email campaigns, and will readily consider automatic monthly contributions if the process is easy for them to set-up and cancel when needed. In addition, your website needs to provide a lot of information about the organization and the impact it is making. Transparency is key.

Organizations need to make their case thoroughly, do it well, and present a clear opportunity for the Gen-Xers to act on. They will give and potentially contribute quite significantly, but they need to know that what their investment of time and money has significant impact, and aligns with their concerns and values.

Millennials are a generation that at times still struggles in certain aspects of their lives. Many are caught between a soft job market and high student loans. Some are still looking to establish themselves professionally and personally, looking to start a career, a family, and getting settled on their own.

Despite all that, Millennials are generally a rather optimistic generation in the sense that they feel, as a whole, that there isn't a problem that could not be tackled and solved. They are the most diverse and most integrated generation of our lifetime. Naturally, social media fundraising and crowd sourcing tends to work best with Millennials.

Millennials value connectedness above all else. Where Gen-Xers want outcomes, Millennials need inclusion. It is less important to them that an organization is 100% successful in achieving their objectives, but it is critical that the organization communicates with Millennial supporters what they did, and how they did it. Millennials value effort and engagement, they won't forgive an organization that makes them feel unneeded, overlooked, or underappreciated.

Millennials feel that they have a lot to offer, and in fact they *do* have a lot to offer. It is up to the organization to meet the needs of this audience. To Millennials, their time and their skills are equally as important as their money – if not more. They may not be able to write a check, but they will give you an afternoon of their time. While Boomers often first connect to an organization by making a gift, Millennials initially connect by volunteering or participating in an event. Special events are important to Millennials, but not the black-tie kind of events. Even if the financial returns aren't immediately coming from this generation, it is vital for the long-term success of any organization to find ways to connect with and nurture their relationship with Millennials. Major gifts are not yet coming from this generation in large numbers – but they will in time. Organizations would do well to be inclusive of Millennials, and position themselves as a part of their lives now.

Let's Talk Marketing

Communication and marketing is not necessarily directly tied to fundraising, but it helps to have an open, collaborative relationship between those two functions of the organization. Marketing typically sells the **now** of an organization, while fundraising and development engages donors with a **vision of what could be**. As a result, fundraising needs to be a strategic extension of any current marketing effort, and both need to be deeply connected to the mission and vision of the organization.

In smaller organizations, fundraising and marketing/communications are often combined into one single job description. That can be good in the sense that fundraising and marketing are definitely on the same page. It can also be bad, because good marketing and communication efforts require planning, execution and time. All that takes away from active donor engagement and fundraising. Some organizations put great value into their annual report and quarterly newsletters. In smaller nonprofits in particular it's worth investigating if the investment of staff time in the creation of these pieces is producing the intended results and return on investment.

Donors need to know that the organization is managing their revenue and expenses appropriately, and how much of their donation is helping make an impact. Some financial reporting by the organization is also legally required. The key is to find a balance between:

- Information that needs to be shared.
- Information that engages donors through stories and inspires donations.
- Pleasing internal stakeholders, but potentially not effectively connecting with external audiences. Internal stakeholders are important, but balance is key.

Some fundraisers opt to eliminate glossy newsletters and annual reports, because the investment in staff time, and print and mailing cost can be substantial. This approach may work for some organizations, but generally speaking a nonprofit with a history of producing certain communication pieces will have a difficult time letting go of those "sacred cows". That doesn't mean publications should continue indefinitely and without review and discussion. Whether the communication is done digitally or in print, through social media or more traditional mechanisms, each piece should be reviewed with the following questions in mind:

- Is the information required to be made available to the public (the organization's annual revenue and expense report being a good example)?
- Can the information be shared or distributed through different means? For example, could the annual report be published on the organization's website instead of mailing it out to key stakeholders and donors?
- Does it need to be produced in print, or can it be done exclusively electronically?
- How does this particular publication or communication channel help connect the organization with various stakeholders?
- Is it reaching the right audience?
- How can we ensure that it reaches the audience we want to reach?
- Do we have permission to contact our intended audience through this channel or with this piece of communication? If not, how do we get permission?
- Does it help us attract new volunteers?
- Does it help us attract new donors and gifts?

These questions are universal and should be considered whether you are looking at your printed annual report, your email newsletter, your Facebook page, or your Twitter account. And even with the rules of social media platforms constantly changing, these questions and considerations generally remain relevant.

Marketing and communication can play a big part in helping reach out to individuals the organization tries to serve, and in attracting new volunteers and donors. A steady stream of information coming from the organization through social media, press releases, and printed materials can also set the stage with current and potential donors. If there is a baseline of understanding about the organization already established, it makes any future conversations between fundraiser and prospective donor that much more substantive. Therefore, any successful nonprofit needs to execute its marketing strategy in close integration with its fundraising program.

Your Fundraising Staff

Newly established and smaller organization often don't have the resources to hire full-time fundraising staff, or any fundraising staff at all. In those cases, that job usually falls on the founder, the executive director, or a few dedicated volunteers and board members. If those individuals don't have a professional background in fundraising, there's the potential that fundraising activities are done at a sub-optimal level. Salary savings are offset by the fact that the executive director now has to give up a portion of their time to perform a role they may not be suited for (or that they don't like performing). As a result, the quality of their mission-related work may be short-changed while the fundraising performance of the organization still suffers.

The problem is trying to pin-point just when the organization should be investing resources into part-time or full-time fundraising staff. There is no formula that states that for every 10,000 donors in the database the organization needs to bring in one part-time fundraiser. There are however some other thresholds worth considering.

If the organization decides to prioritize their fundraising without bringing in additional staff, I would strongly recommend that the board set aside some professional development funds to coach up the staff member designated to take on fundraising responsibilities. Paying for one membership with the Association of Fundraising Professionals is very affordable, and it allows for access to numerous online resources, local networking events with other fundraising professionals, and reduced fees for online workshops. It's an investment the organization will recoup quickly just by optimizing existing programs, and following best practices.

If the organization has the option to invest a little bit more money (without hiring additional staff), The Fund Raising School at Lilly Family School of Philanthropy at Indiana University offers an array of fundraising courses for professionals at all stages in their career. Courses are hosted in several major cities in the continental U.S., and absolutely worth the price of tuition.

As an alternative, the organization could opt to bring in a fundraising consultant to specifically analyze and optimize the existing fundraising program at the organization, and coach up the staff. Having this kind of customized training may turn out to be the best return on investment for the organization without taking the step to hire a professional full or part-time fundraiser just yet.

There are some indicators and scenarios when a nonprofit should absolutely consider bringing a professional fundraiser into the organization.

- **The organization wants to launch a capital campaign:** provided a feasibility study has been completed and all signs are positive that the campaign stands a chance of succeeding, bringing in a dedicated fundraiser is critical.
- **The organization has between 50 to 100 high-level prospects who would require regular engagement before becoming major gift donors:** a full-time major gift fundraiser typically carries a portfolio of 80 to 120 prospects, and will make around 15 face-to-face visits per month (this may vary slightly from organization to organization, but those numbers are fairly typical industry benchmarks for dedicated major gift fundraisers). If an organization has at least 40 to 60 prospects, a part-time Director of Development will be very much worth the investment.
- **The organization wants to increase revenue from grants, special events, or corporate sponsorships:** all of those activities depend on a fair amount of staff time, and it is unlikely that these activities can be managed effectively by simply adding them to somebody's existing full-time job requirements.

If one or more of these scenarios apply, the organization has reached the point when a strategic investment to hire dedicated fundraising staff should be given serious consideration. When that time comes, begin by looking at suggested job descriptions, which can be found on the websites of the Association of Fundraising Professionals (AFP: www.afpnet.org) or the Council for the Advancement and Support of Education (CASE: www.case.org). In addition, bringing in a fundraising consultant can help your organization, your executive director, and your board conduct a successful hiring process the first time around.

A Word About Performance-based Pay

Whether your organization is working with a fundraising consultant or a paid fundraiser on your staff, there is one guideline that should always be adhered to: *there should never be a performance bonus awarded for achieving or exceeding fundraising goals*. While there is no law prohibiting performance-based bonuses, the Association of Fundraising Professionals and other professional associations have adopted strict ethical guidelines specifically addressing this issue.

A fundraiser first and foremost needs to represent the organization, and the mission and interests of the organization. Any performance-based pay undermines that relationship.

Rather than working for the betterment of the organization, the fundraiser now works for their self-interest. This can potentially have devastating consequences for the long-term relationship between the organization and their supporters. A fundraiser working toward performance bonuses is easily tempted to push harder for a major commitment from the donor than the donor might otherwise be comfortable with. This could turn goodwill toward the mission of the organization into a serious case of buyer's remorse, or worse compromise the donor's financial well-being and the long-term prospects of the organization's fundraising program.

The only exception to this rule is if the organization has standard practices for performance-based increases in place that apply to all staff. Example: at the end of the fiscal year, the board of directors approves a 1% salary increase for all employees. In addition, the board sets aside some funding so that a small handful of outstanding employees may receive an additional 1% merit increase for exceptional work in the prior fiscal year. Only under those conditions should fundraising staff ever be considered for a performance-based increase. Otherwise, there should *never* be bonuses or percentage payouts being made for raising a certain gift amount. There should never be an agreement in place granting fundraisers a percentage of any gift going to the organization. The same applies to outside consultants. Similarly, if a part-time fundraisers puts in the time to research and write a grant application, the fundraiser needs to be compensated at a previously agreed upon rate – not if and when the grant request gets funded.

While these types of performance bonuses or sales commissions are standard practice in the corporate sector, it is never permissible to implement them in the nonprofit sector. Board members with a corporate background may push the organization to adopt a performance-based pay model in lieu of a higher set salary for the fundraising staff. It is in the best interest of the organization and its relationship to its donors to categorically reject those ideas.

Working with Consultants

The nonprofit sector has whole cottage industry of consultants and for-profit companies offering products and services to support fundraising. Consultants cost money, and in some cases quite a lot of money. This can result in sticker shock so severe that some nonprofits simply opt not to make that investment. Sometimes, this is the right decision. At other times, shying away from making the necessary investments can harm the organization in the long run.

Example: nonprofits of a certain size are required to file a detailed tax return, IRS Form 990. For some organizations, this can be a very simple process. For others, it can be a source of significant headaches. In those cases, nonprofits often turn to a professional to help prepare their tax documents, because it's more efficient. Doing it wrong could end up being very costly – both in additional hours spent, or in extra costs incurred to correct mistakes later on. The decision to contract with professionals for those types of services is usually not questioned by the board.

With fundraising consultants, the situation often feels fundamentally different. The organization wants to raise money, not spend it. The board doesn't want to see a huge outlay of cash before a single dime is raised. Those feelings are valid, but they are just that: an emotional response to something that needs be treated objectively. Here is my checklist for why it might make sense to bring in a fundraising consultant:

- The time you might spend addressing an issue would cost your organization more in salary than it would cost to pay the consultant who could do it quicker, more effectively, and correctly the first time around.
- Bringing in a consultant could lead to in-house staff acquiring new skills and expertise, which would save the organization money and increase fundraising revenue down the road.
- Some volunteers and some board members want to know that you have brought together the best people you can to work on a project. This instills trust in your organization, which builds confidence in the overall effort. That confidence and trust then leads to larger gifts.

If you are serious about achieving your goals, don't pinch pennies during the planning stages. Consultants can be very much worth the investment if you know what you are getting into. A few more things worth considering:

- Be very clear about expectations: what do you need to accomplish? By when? How much money can you spend, not just on the consultant but on the overall project as well? I know this is a well-worn expression, but in fundraising, and especially in capital campaign fundraising, this is absolutely true: the organization needs to spend some money to make money. If the organization is unprepared or unwilling to shoulder significant expenses, then it is not yet ready to proceed. If that's the case, the first step may be to fundraise for capacity building, which the organization can then re-invest into its larger campaign.

- Put everything in writing, including what happens if there are delays, or if the organization needs more help than initially anticipated. Everything should be clearly laid out in the Request for Proposal (RFP), and then verified against the consulting agreement before signing it.
- Lastly, and this is a big one, fundraising consultants usually *do not* fundraise *for* you. Period. They will put together a plan for you to execute, and they will (depending on your agreement with them) help you carry out the plan, train staff and volunteers, and monitor performance. Consultants can help raise hundreds of thousands, or even millions of dollars for the organization, but the key word is *help*. Always be very clear about what you expect of your fundraising consultants, and what they can expect of you.

Final Thoughts

Final Thoughts

Fundraising is one of the most exciting aspects of nonprofit work, because it allows volunteers and staff fundraisers to make a meaningful impact in a very tangible way. We are usually drawn to an organization, because their mission overlaps with our own interests and values. Being able to help an organization get closer to fulfilling their mission also fulfills a part of ourselves. Helping a nonprofit succeed is an incredibly rewarding experience.

While there are different ways of helping a nonprofit, the most impactful way is by securing the financial resources they need to do their work. Concluding a successful campaign can be life-changing: for the volunteers and staff, but first and foremost for the people the organization is trying to help. You have the opportunity to participate in something that can have impact for decades: the first generation college student who is able to get a degree because of the financial support from scholarships. The homeless mother who just needed a break and resources and guidance to get back on her feet. The after-school reading program that finally allowed a six year-old child to feel like he was smart. A playground that was saved with the support of an entire community.

Fundraising is a noble profession and a worthwhile task, because it is done in services of others. We as fundraisers invite donors to share a part of themselves for the benefit of the greater good. It is about creating opportunities and forming connections. It is about opening doors where there were none. It is about hope. It is about second chances. It is a labor of love, and we are privileged to be a part of it.

ABOUT THE AUTHOR

Marc Huber has been a fundraising professional since 1998, working for several mid-sized and national nonprofits, including the Rotary International Foundation, the American Library Association, and Indiana University-Purdue University Indianapolis (IUPUI). In addition, he has provided fundraising consulting services to a number of organizations since 2013, helping those organizations raise over $5 million during that time span.

Marc Huber has a long track record of running campaigns that increased the number of donors and overall giving, and has been involved in creating campaign strategies and materials for annual, capital, and planned giving campaigns. He has conducted fundraising training seminars for volunteers, and collaborated with volunteer leaders on major gift asks.

Marc Huber is available for strategic advice, board and volunteer training, assessments of campaigns and programs, and direct support for planned and ongoing fundraising initiatives.

Visit **www.fundraisingcopilot.com** for more information.

www.ingramcontent.com/pod-product-compliance
Lightning Source LLC
Chambersburg PA
CBHW061441180526
45170CB00004B/1509